# The Latest in Recycling

### by Charlotte Larsen

HOUGHTON MIFFLIN          BOSTON

PHOTOGRAPHY CREDITS
**Cover** © Fotopic/Index Stock Imagery; **1** © Kim Karpeles/Alamy; **2** © Mary Kate Denny/PhotoEdit; **5** © Kim Karpeles/Alamy; **7** © Digital Vision/PunchStock; **9** © Mark Boulton/Alamy

Printed in China

ISBN 10: 0-618-89932-4
ISBN 13: 978-0-618-89932-6

23456789 NOR 16 15 14 13 12 11 10 09 08

After you drink a bottle of water, what do you do with the plastic bottle? You have two choices: throw it in the trash or recycle it. Here is why you should recycle:

- Recycling saves energy. It usually takes a lot less energy to make something out of recycled material than to make something out of new material.

- Recycling saves our natural resources. Natural resources are things we get from Earth, such as plants, land, minerals, and water.

- Recycling can cut down on pollution—dirt in the air and water. For example, reusing metal from old cans to make more cans is a lot cleaner than making cans from new metal.

As you can see, recycling is good for our planet! So what is going on with recycling these days? Is it really making a difference? Let's check the facts. In 1990, 90% of all trash was burned or put into landfills. Only 10% was recycled. In 2005, 32% of the 245.7 million tons of garbage we made was recycled. That's a big step in the right direction!

Look at the chart below to see how the percentage of recycled trash, or solid waste, has increased over the last 40 years.

| Where Trash Has Gone, 1970–2005 (in percent of total waste) | | | | | |
|---|---|---|---|---|---|
| | 1970 | 1980 | 1990 | 2000 | 2005 |
| Trash put in landfills | 93.1% | 88.6% | 63.9% | 56.7% | 54.3% |
| Trash burned to create energy | 0.3% | 1.8% | 14.5% | 14.2% | 13.6% |
| Trash recycled | 6.6% | 9.6% | 16.2% | 29.1% | 32.1% |

**Read·Think·Write** Compare the data for 1970 with the data for 2005. How much more trash was recycled in 2005 than in 1970?

The amount of 245.7 million tons is a lot of trash! Look at the circle graph below to see what makes up this country's garbage.

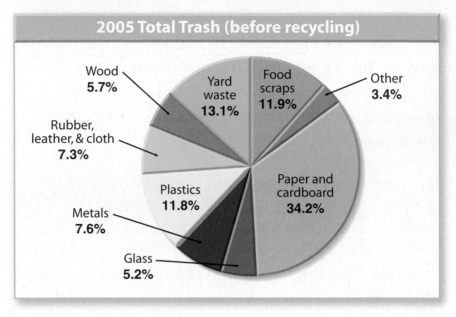

**2005 Total Trash (before recycling)**

Wood 5.7%
Yard waste 13.1%
Food scraps 11.9%
Other 3.4%
Rubber, leather, & cloth 7.3%
Plastics 11.8%
Paper and cardboard 34.2%
Metals 7.6%
Glass 5.2%

You can see on the chart that many things people throw away can be recycled. Glass, paper, metals (such as food and drink cans), and plastics are valuable materials that are easily recycled.

Other kinds of waste, such as yard waste and food scraps, can be composted. During composting, living bacteria and fungi break down natural wastes, including old food, cut grass, and tree leaves. Composting turns waste into a material that can be used to help make soil better for growing plants.

Although much of our trash can be recycled, not everyone is recycling. Out of 84 million tons of paper that Americans threw away in 2005, only 42 million tons were recycled. Only 25% of glass containers and 29% of plastic bottles were recycled that year.

Some cities have curbside recycling, with trucks to pick up glass, plastic, paper, and cans. People in these places do the most recycling.

Some experts think that if every city in the United States had curbside recycling, we would reduce the amount of solid waste by 15% to 25%.

**Read·Think·Write** What percentage of paper that was thrown away in 2005 was recycled?

# Recycling Paper

Believe it or not, paper takes up more room than anything else in landfills. Newspapers, magazines, and other kinds of paper fill more than 40% of landfill space! Paper does not break down well inside a landfill. It just sits there year after year.

Many people feel that we do not recycle and reuse enough of our paper. Most of the time we cut down trees to make more paper instead of using recycled paper.

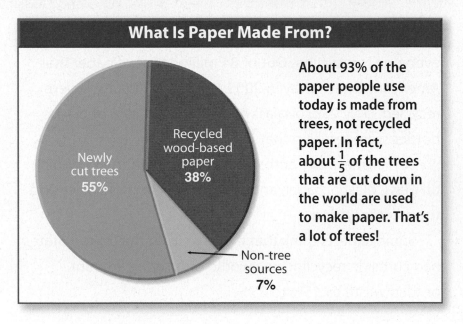

**What Is Paper Made From?**

Recycled wood-based paper
38%

Newly cut trees
55%

Non-tree sources
7%

About 93% of the paper people use today is made from trees, not recycled paper. In fact, about $\frac{1}{5}$ of the trees that are cut down in the world are used to make paper. That's a lot of trees!

**Read·Think·Write** Use the circle graph to find what percentage of paper is made from newly cut trees.

It is easy to make new paper using recycled paper. Waste paper is mixed with pulp, which is wet, mushy wood from new trees. Any ink that was left on the old paper is taken out of the mixture. Then the mixture is colored, pressed into a thin layer, dried, rolled, and cut.

Using recycled paper to make new paper makes sense. Recycling paper puts less trash in our landfills. Making new paper from recycled paper also puts less pollution into our air and water and uses less energy. That makes the world a healthier place.

In 2003, the United States reached its goal of recycling 50% of all its paper. The new goal is to recycle 55% of all our paper by 2012.

**Read·Think·Write** If there are 80 million tons of waste paper in 2012, how many tons would the United States need to recycle to meet its newest recycling goal?

# Recycling Plastics

In the United States we use lots of plastic! We make clothes, shoes, pens, cups, chairs, rulers, and much more out of plastic.

There are many kinds of plastic. Drink bottles are made of one kind of plastic, called PET plastic. Milk jugs are made of another kind of plastic, called HDPE plastic. Straws and yogurt cups are made of PP plastic. Each kind of plastic usually has to be separated when it is recycled.

Americans are not recycling much plastic. Look at the chart below to see how many thousands of tons of plastics were made in 2005. Then look at how much of that plastic was recycled.

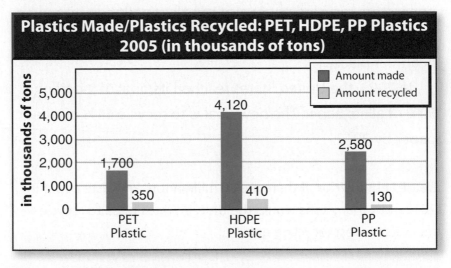

**Read·Think·Write** Estimate the percentage of PET plastics that are recycled.

**A plastic lumber chair like this one was made from 240 recycled milk jugs! It is waterproof, as hard as wood, and will not crack or rot like regular wood.**

The good news is that recycled plastic can be used in many different ways. Drink bottles made of PET plastic can be melted down and used to make shirts, carpet, and, of course, more drink bottles.

Recycled HDPE plastic can be used to make plastic wood, or lumber. This lumber can be used instead of wood to make tables and chairs, running paths, and railroad ties.

One major car company has even used millions of pounds of recycled plastic to make engine parts, car window parts, and car carpeting. Now that's great recycling!

# Recycling Metal

Cans, cans, and more cans! Every day, Americans use millions of metal cans—200 million aluminum drink cans and 100 million steel food cans. But only about 45% of the drink cans and 63% of the food cans get recycled. The rest go into landfills.

Recycling aluminum and steel saves a lot of energy. Making 1 pound of new aluminum takes 7.5 kilowatt hours of electricity. Making 1 pound of recycled aluminum from old cans takes only 4% of that energy. The same thing is true with steel. It takes 60% less energy to make steel from recycled steel than it does to make steel from new materials. So just rinse and recycle those used cans. It's that easy!

**Read·Think·Write** How many kilowatt hours of electricity does it take to make 1 pound of recycled aluminum from old cans?

For paper, plastic, metal, and glass, recycling is the key to saving energy and reducing the percentage of trash that goes into landfills. It makes a big difference!

So what can we recycle, and how do we do it? Take a look at the chart below and remember to recycle!

| What Can We Recycle? | | |
|---|---|---|
| Material | Examples | How to Do It |
| Paper | Newspapers, telephone books, cardboard boxes, white office paper, egg cartons | Keep the papers clean and dry. |
| Plastics | Water and juice bottles, 2-liter soda bottles, milk jugs | Separate the different kinds of plastics. Rinse them out. |
| Aluminum | Foil, pie pans, drink cans | Rinse them out and crush them. |
| Steel | Cans from soup, tuna, and other foods | Rinse them out and crush them. |
| Glass | Clear, green, and brown bottles and jars | Rinse them out, take off their lids, and separate them by color. |

**Read·Think·Write** If the percentage of trash that goes into landfills is reduced through recycling, what happens to the percentage of trash that is recycled?

1. **Predict Outcomes** What is 25% of 360?

2. About $\frac{1}{5}$ of the trees that are cut down in the world are used to make paper. What percentage of trees is this?

3. Look at the data below. They show how many pounds of glass, plastic, paper, and cans were collected at Copeland School, for a total of 210 pounds of recyclables. Make a circle graph that shows in percents the amount of each material that was collected.

| Recyclable Material | Pounds Collected |
|:---:|:---:|
| glass | 40 |
| plastic | 20 |
| paper | 80 |
| cans | 70 |

## Activity

Use fraction circles to show the following percentages.

Circle 1: 50%, 20%, 30%

Circle 2: 25%, 25%, 20%, 10%, 10%, 10%

Circle 3: 33.3%, 33.3%, 33.3%